Natural Disasters

Natural Disasters:

Unleashing the Fury of Nature

Martin Holden and Karen Holden

A FRIEDMAN GROUP BOOK

Copyright © 1995 by Michael Friedman Publishing Group, Inc.

ISBN 0-8317-6318-3

NATURAL DISASTERS
was prepared and produced by
Michael Friedman Publishing Group, Inc.
15 West 26th Street
New York, New York 10010

Editor: Sharon Kalman
Designer: Robert W. Kosturko
Photography Editor: Christopher C. Bain
Photo Researcher: Daniella Jo Nilva
Production Manager: Karen L. Greenberg

Typeset by BPE Graphics, Inc.
Color separations by Kwong Ming Graphicprint Co., Ltd.
Printed in China by Leefung-Asco Printers Ltd.

. . . but the truly noble and resolved spirit raises itself, and becomes more

CONTENTS

© Carol Simowitz

INTRODUCTION

THE WORD *DISASTER* COMES FROM THE LATIN PHRASE for ill-starred, or the product of unhappy fate. This reflects the way people around the world still think of the disasters that threaten them. Although unfortunate and even tragic, disasters are impersonal and inevitable, and there is little to gain from worrying about them. Medieval scholars tried to depict disasters as the result of God's wrath, like dress rehearsals for Judgement Day. Later, it was fashionable to consider them subversions of the otherwise symmetrical natural order of the Universe. Most people, however, continued to believe that disasters were written in the stars.

Science has reinforced the notion of inevitability on the one hand, while undermining it on the other. The more we study disasters of all kinds, the more they appear to form patterns. What once appeared to be capricious events, such as El Niño, now seem to be part of a comprehensible system. Even as we grow to accept the inevitability of earthquakes, cyclones, and volcanic eruptions, we prepare for them, reducing their potency as disasters. A violent earthquake is not a disaster if buildings have been designed to withstand it and refuse to fall down.

More and more the developed world is denying the Grim Reaper his accustomed binges. In the United States and Europe the death toll from all kinds of disasters declines each year. However, the financial toll is on the rise, not only because of inflation, but also because we accumulate more

© Ann & Myron Sutton/FPG International

buildings and property each year. In the so-called developing countries, the story is very different. The ever increasing concentration of people in shantytowns has led to an increasing rate of disaster fatalities. Droughts and floods that once killed thousands now kill tens of thousands.

In the pages that follow, the two major groups of natural disasters will be explored, those caused by the restlessness of the earth beneath us, and those originating in the turbulent atmosphere overhead. We will see why earthquakes and volcanic eruptions occur where they do, and how their violence stems from the relentless movement of the earth's great crustal plates. We will learn how deadly hurricanes and typhoons are born, and investigate the mysterious and unpredictable behavior of tornadoes. Then we will see how disasters can occur on a global scale, affecting all parts of the world in different ways, when the delicate balance between the ocean and atmosphere is disrupted.

Disasters interest us on many different levels, from morbid fascination to dispassionate scientific study. The awesome strength that nature is able to muster so casually serves to remind us of our own fragility and of the transience of life on earth. Sometimes we need to be reminded.

Mt. St. Helens in Washington State, after the eruption of May 18, 1980. This view (left), from the once densely forested Windy Ridge, shows the new shape of the volcano after it lost more than 1000 feet (365 meters) of its elevation in the explosion. Note the trees' trunks pointing away from the volcano, and the plants which are beginning to take root in the volcanic ash.

The Guatemalan earthquake of 1976 was one of the worst disasters to occur in the Western Hemisphere, taking 24,000 lives and leaving as many as one million people homeless. These children (right), standing amid the rubble of their village, symbolize both the unbearable tragedy of disaster and the indominable hope that allows the survivors to carry on.

Chapter One

EARTHQUAKES

AT 5:35 P.M. ON MARCH 27, 1964, LIFE must have looked pretty good to the people of Anchorage, Alaska. The working week was over, and Easter weekend was about to begin. There was even a hint of spring in the air. But at 5:36, everyone's weekend plans were suddenly changed. A low rumble slowly became audible, and the ground trembled underfoot. Then the earth began to undulate in great swells, knocking houses from their foundations, toppling buildings, and buckling the streets. This continued for four minutes.

Like many cities, Anchorage is built on an unstable mixture of mud and sand. During the earthquake, much of this material lost all cohesion and liquefied. The effect was like that of a tablecloth yanked inexpertly from under a china setting: total destruction. Thirty blocks of the city were flattened. The ground opened up in gaping fissures, swallowing houses, cars, and small children.

In the ports of Seward and Valdez, more than 100 miles (160 kilometers) apart at opposite ends of Prince William Sound, the frightened residents had barely gotten to their feet when they saw an enormous tsunami (an unusually large wave caused by displacement of the sea floor) looming over the water. Ships at anchor were plucked from the harbor and hurled into shops and factories. Many small fishing villages were obliterated. The tsunami raced across the Pacific at 400 miles (640 kilometers) per hour, drowning unsuspecting bathers on the coasts of northern California and Oregon.

With a Richter magnitude of 8.3, the quake was the most powerful to ever strike North America. The earth was warped over an area of 200,000 square miles (518,000 square kilometers), in some places by as much as thirty feet (nine meters). Since it struck in an area of relatively sparse population, the earthquake's toll was mercifully light.

© AP/Wide World Photos

© Gene Daniels/Black Star

During the 1964 Alaskan earthquake, fifteen people were swept to their deaths and the fishing industry was all but destroyed when a series of tsunamis swamped the fishing village of Kodiak (above). Anchorage's Fourth Avenue (right) shifted twenty feet (six meters) during the earthquake. The Anchorage suburb of Turnagain Heights (left) was built on unstable sediment that liquefied during the earthquake, destroying the town almost completely.

© Reuters/Bettmann NewsPhotos

Earthquakes result from the constant jostling of the dozen or so rigid plates that make up the earth's crust. Along the mid-ocean ridges, or spreading centers, magma (volcanic material) rising from the semi-molten mantle below pushes these plates outward, while at their far edges they grind against or slide under others. The plates do not move smoothly past one another, but are held together by friction where they come into contact. The pressure on the plate boundary, or fault, continues to build until it is released as an earthquake.

The spot where the friction is first overcome is called the *focus*. When an earthquake strikes, the stored energy is released as intense seismic vibrations, which travel outward from the focus in all directions. These vibrations, or waves, have different properties, and have been assigned different names by seismologists. *Compressional waves* (also known as *P waves*) compress the rock in front of them and extend it behind them as they pass through the earth, moving like a caterpillar, but much faster—about four miles (six kilometers) per second. *Shear waves* (or *S waves*) travel at half the speed of P waves, undulating through the earth like ocean swells. These two kinds of waves interact to form *surface waves,* which cause the greatest damage to structures.

The magnitude of earthquakes is measured using the Richter scale, which is based on the amplitude of these waves as recorded by a seismograph. The tremors are recorded on a constantly rotating scroll by the vibrations of a delicate stylus. The graphs produced on this device are measured, then interpreted using a simple formula which takes into account the distance between the seismograph and the focus of the earthquakes.

The resulting numbers are based on a logarithmic scale, meaning that an increase of one unit implies a tenfold increase in the magnitude of the earthquake. An earthquake of magnitude 8, for example, is 10,000 times greater than one of magnitude 4. This reflects the fact that the few large earthquakes that strike each year release far more energy than do the approximately 800,000 small earthquakes that occur over the same time period. Earthquakes of magnitude 5 or above are capable of doing visible damage, and at magnitude 8 or higher the damage is almost total.

The surfaces along which the earth's crustal plates meet are generally known as *faults,* although many smaller faults are found in the interior of plates as well. The longest faults are those that offset the mid-ocean ridges, known as *transform faults*. Twenty million years ago, the mid-ocean ridge in the Eastern Pacific was overrun by the North American Plate, which was then split apart along one of the ridge's transform faults. The fault still connects spreading centers and forms the eastern boundary of the Pacific plate, but now passes

through the continental crust—as California's San Andreas Fault. Since the fault was captured, Southern California has migrated more than 350 miles (560 kilometers) north along it. That entire distance was traveled in inches or several feet at a time, during earthquakes.

In Northern California, the San Andreas Fault runs between the steep, redwood-shrouded slopes of the Santa Cruz Mountains and the San Francisco Bay, disappearing beneath the Pacific Ocean north of the Golden Gate Bridge. On the afternoon of October 17, 1989, almost 60,000 Bay Area baseball fans were gathered in Candlestick Park for the third game of the World Series. As the Oakland A's and the San Francisco Giants were warming up, and the announcers reeled off their pregame prattle, the television audience saw the field begin to shake violently before the image suddenly blinked off. It was not a case of bad reception.

At that moment, the entire Bay Area was shaken by a powerful earthquake centered near the otherwise peaceful seaside resort

Street scenes show the results of the earthquake of April 18, 1906, which destroyed 38,000 buildings in San Francisco. Electrical, gas, and water lines were cut by the initial shock, setting the stage for the even more catastrophic fires that followed. This is a view of San Francisco taken from a "captive airship," with Market Street crossing the center of the picture (following pages). The large building in the foreground is the U.S. Mint, which held $200 million in gold bullion at the time of the earthquake and was protected by its own detachment of troops. It still stands, one of the few major buildings to survive the disaster.

Flames spread through buildings in San Francisco's Marina District, damaged in the earthquake of October 17, 1989 (below), eerily reminiscent of the great earthquake and fire of 1906. Although the destruction was less widespread and the fires were quickly controlled, some San Franciscans learned that their damaged homes would be bulldozed in the quake's aftermath (right).

In the worst single tragedy of the 1989 Northern California Earthquake, a mile (one-and-a-half kilometers) of the upper level of Oakland's Nimitz Freeway collapsed, crushing dozens of commuters (far right).

and university town of Santa Cruz, 70 miles (110 kilometers) south of San Francisco. The unreinforced brick buildings that lined the town's historic Garden Mall shuddered and collapsed onto pedestrians and parked cars in the street below. A wall that moments before had held the attention of browsers in the children's section of a bookshop tumbled onto the employees of the coffee roasting company next door. In seconds the vibrant heart of Santa Cruz was reduced to rubble.

The earthquake wrought havoc all around the Bay. In San Francisco's Marina District entire blocks of homes and apartments were destroyed when the unstable landfill on which they had been built became liquefied. Rush-hour traffic on the Bay Bridge ground to a halt as a section of the upper level fell through—one car teetering precipitously on the brink as its terrified occupants scrambled out through the windows. Less fortunate were the motorists taking Oakland's Nimitz Freeway home that evening; dozens were crushed to death when a mile-long section of the upper roadway collapsed onto their vehicles.

With a Richter magnitude of 6.9, the Santa Cruz earthquake of 1989 was the worst disaster to strike the region since the legendary San Francisco earthquake of 1906—which had an estimated magnitude of 8.3. The 1906 earthquake shook San Francisco, as one contemporary observer put it, "Like a terrier shaking a rat." The damage was enhanced by the fact that much of the city was (and is) built on unstable sediments, and by the catastrophic fires which swept through the ruins afterward. The Federal Government has estimated that if an earthquake similar in size to San Francisco's were to strike the Los Angeles region, up to 23,000 people would be killed by it and two million left homeless.

Other earthquake faults are formed where continents collide. The Caucasus

With the help of specially trained dogs, rescuers searched in the rubble of Leninakan, USSR for possible survivors following the earthquake of December 7, 1988 (below). A building in Leninakan stands exposed to the elements after a wall tumbled into the street below (right). One of the 25,000 victims of the Armenian Earthquake rests amid the ruins of a partially destroyed apartment complex (far right).

Mountains in Soviet Armenia rose where the Arabian Plate pushes northward against the Russian Platform, squeezing Turkey and Iran out to either side. This boundary is marked by a number of large faults, one of which produced an earthquake of magnitude 7 on December 7, 1988. The ground on one side of the fault leapt up suddenly to form a four-foot- (one-meter-) high scarp, expelling scorching vapors which caused adjacent bushes to burst into flame. God did not speak from the burning bushes, but the message was clear nonetheless.

The city of Spitak was completely destroyed. Half of nearby Leninakan was lost as well. Thousands of people were trapped under the concrete rubble, slowly dying as the authorities searched for the heavy equipment needed to clear the debris. With the help of thousands of Soviet soldiers and military doctors, as well as a dramatic outpouring of international aid, 15,000 people were eventually plucked from the rubble alive. However, 25,000 people were killed, and 500,000 survivors were left to face the approaching snows without a home.

Where an oceanic plate dips down under the edge of another plate, deep earthquakes are formed. These tremors are focused on the upper surface of the descending plate, a region called the *Benioff Zone.* The catastrophic earthquakes that rock the islands of Japan and the west coast of South America originate in this zone, as did the Alaskan earthquake of 1964.

One of these deep-seated tremors, measuring 7.75 on the Richter scale, flattened much of northern Peru on May 30, 1970. It sent a landslide of ninety million cubic yards (sixty-nine million cubic meters) of rock and snow roaring 12,000 feet (3,700 meters) down the face of Peru's highest peak, Nevado de Huascaran, into several lakes at the mountain's base. People in the towns of Yungay and Ranrahirca in the valley below were still reeling from the earthquake when they looked up to see one hundred million cubic yards

In Peru's Rio Santa Valley (left), the tops of a few palm trees mark the spot where the town of Yungay and its 20,000 inhabitants lie buried under some 40 feet (12 meters) of landslide debris. The remains of a building (below) were reduced to rubble during the Peruvian earthquake of 1970. Survivors begin the arduous task of rebuilding (right).

(seventy-seven million cubic meters) of mud bearing down on them at almost 200 miles (320 kilometers) per hour. Twenty-five thousand were buried alive.

Although most earthquakes occur along the margins of the crustal plates, the interiors of the continents are by no means immune. Faults lie under all parts of North America, gradually accumulating stress over thousands of years; many of them have produced very serious earthquakes. In fact, the most prolonged series of earthquakes in American history was centered

© Fred Ward/Black Star

in northeastern Arkansas. From December 1811 to February 1812, more than a thousand tremors shook the Mississippi Valley, some strong enough to be felt in Boston, Massachusetts, and Washington, D.C. The changes in the land were dramatic. The course of the Mississippi was altered in many places; one jolt made part of the river flow north for a while, before it turned back again to form a series of waterfalls. Land subsidence formed several swamps and lakes, including Reelfoot Lake in Tennessee.

Efforts to predict earthquakes have produced mixed results, but research continues. Because the strain on faults is known to produce warping of the earth's surface, networks of sensitive measuring devices have been installed across dangerous faults like the San Andreas. Seismologists are also studying the patterns of foreshocks that sometimes precede large earthquakes, to determine if these can be used for prediction. Scientists in Italy and China are investigating the strange behavior many animals seem to display before

an earthquake strikes in hopes of determining what it is that the animals sense.

Can earthquakes be prevented? Recent studies suggest that this fantastic notion could become a reality. The injection of waste fluids into deep wells along an active fault in Colorado was shown to have stimulated its gradual movement. The future may see faults such as the San Andreas lined with "lubrication wells," which might cause the movement along the fault to occur as a series of constant, short slips—instead of the Big One.

VOLCANOES

SET LIKE A GEM BENEATH THE VER-
dant mountains of Martinique's west coast,
the cosmopolitan city of St. Pierre was often spoken of as the Paris of the West Indies. Above the pretty whitewashed buildings and red-tiled roofs rose the dramatic
peak of Mt. Pelée, its lake-filled summit crater favored for picnicking, swimming, and
watching the sun set over the Caribbean.
In April 1902, the narrow streets of St.
Pierre were awash with colorful bougainvil-
lea blossoms and political posters. The
newly-founded Radical Party, representing
Martinique's black and mulatto majority,
had issued a challenge to the ruling Prog-

ress Party of Governor Mouttet. The election was slated for May 10.

In early April, Mt. Pelée began to rumble and expel clouds of ash and noxious
fumes from its summit crater, reminding
the people below that they did indeed live
under a volcano. As the fumes became
stronger and the ash deepened in the narrow streets, the residents of St. Pierre began to worry. But no one was as worried
as Governor Mouttet, who was concerned
that the flight of prosperous residents
would hand the upcoming election to the
Radicals. Newspaper editors obligingly
played down the threat of an eruption,

even blaming the growing panic on Radical agitation.

On May 3, a fissure rent the flank of Mt.
Pelée, discharging a hot, viscous mix of
ash and mud, destroying a mountain village and a sugar plantation before hurtling
down the Roxelane River, which flowed
through the city's center. The American
consul drafted a telegram to Washington,
but it was intercepted by Mouttet, who
sent his own wire to Paris claiming that the
eruption was subsiding. As ash continued
to rain down, collapsing roofs and filling
the streets, Mouttet was obliged to post
soldiers on the roads to keep the elector-

The city of St. Pierre, Martinique lies at the foot of cloud-wreathed Mt. Peleé (far left). This photo was taken a few years before its destruction in 1902. A *nueé ardente* like the one that struck St. Pierre cascades down the slopes of Mt. Peleé (left) later the same year. The clothing of this victim, lying amid the ruins of the Military Hospital (above), was vaporized by the intense heat of the eruption.

ate in the city. On May 7, the volcano Soufriére on the nearby island of St. Vincent erupted, killing nearly 2,000 people. The authorities in St. Pierre were reassured by this, reasoning that the pressure on their own volcano must have been relieved. Indeed, Mt. Pelée appeared to grow quiet.

Shortly before 8:00 the next morning, a telegraph operator in nearby Fort-de-France received the signal to transmit from his counterpart in St. Pierre. "*Allez.*" Then the line went dead.

At that moment, several earsplitting explosions rocked Mt. Pelée, and a black cloud, shot through with lightning, billowed out of the crater. At the same time, another cloud burst, rushing down the slopes of the volcano at sixty miles (ninety-six kilometers) per hour toward the city. In seconds, St. Pierre was engulfed in a maelstrom of steam, volatile gases, and ash heated to 1300°F (700°C). The entire city burst into flames, and its 30,000 residents were literally boiled alive as their bodily fluids vaporized in the intense heat. Hundreds of casks that had been sitting on the docks exploded, spreading thousands of gallons of flaming rum across the water, toward ships already aflame in the harbor. Governor Mouttet, who had arrived the day before from Fort-de-France to boost morale, died with his constituency.

As the volcano gently buried the ruins under a coating of ash, would-be rescuers arrived from Fort-de-France in search of survivors. They found only two, one a man lucky enough to have been on the very outskirts of the city, and Auguste Ciparis, a convicted murderer awaiting execution in an underground dungeon. He had been sentenced to die on the morning of the eruption, but his captors never came for him. His original sentence was commuted, and he traveled for years with the Barnum and Bailey Circus in a replica of his cell. It is not known whether or not he was a registered voter.

The searing avalanche of volcanic gases and debris that destroyed St. Pierre is known as a *nuée ardente,* or glowing cloud. Volcanoes produce an amazing amount of gases, particularly water vapor, but also carbon and sulfur dioxides, chlorine, nitrogen, and others. (The volcano of Paricutín, which rose out of a Mexican cornfield in 1943, emitted 18,000 tons [16,000 metric tons] of water vapor per day.) Because this mixture is heavier than the surrounding air, a *nuée ardente* flows downslope. It travels quickly and quietly on a layer of compressed air, incinerating everything in its path. This type of eruption is particularly common in the Caribbean and around the Pacific Ocean, where the rocks fused to produce the volcanic magma contain high concentrations of water.

The steam pressure created when seawater or groundwater percolates down into the molten heart of a volcano can cause the most violent eruptions of all, *phreatic explosions.* The loudest sound ever heard on earth was produced on the morning of August 27, 1883, when a phreatic explosion destroyed the island of Krakatoa in the Sunda Strait between Java and Sumatra. The sound blew out windows and cracked walls on those islands, and was heard nearly 3,000 miles (4,800 kilometers) away. Five square miles (thirteen square kilometers) of rock was ejected, and the ocean rushed into a 1,000-foot- (300-meter-) deep hole where the volcano had once stood 1,000 feet (300 meters) above the sea. Much of the debris was lofted into the atmosphere, where it darkened skies around the world for weeks. Tsunamis as high as 130 feet (thirty-nine meters) swept the Sunda Strait, drowning 36,000 people.

The island of Thera in the Aegean Sea experienced an even greater phreatic explosion around 1470 B.C., which may have provided the basis for the legend of the lost city of Atlantis. The destruction

wrought throughout the Mediterranean by the ensuing tsunamis can only be imagined; many scholars feel that this disaster permanently crippled the once powerful Minoan civilization.

More evidence that volcanoes and water do not mix well comes in the form of *lahars.* These are massive flows of volcanic debris and water, which are endemic to the many volcanoes with water-filled craters, snowcapped summits, or simply rain-saturated flanks. Lahars can transform an otherwise innocuous emission of steam and ash into a roaring torrent of destruction. Mt. Rainier in the state of Washington has produced several enormous lahars over the last few thousand years, covering large areas which are now quite densely populated.

On the night of November 13, 1985, the icy summit of Nevado del Ruiz in Colombia was partially melted by a massive eruption, which was expected by geologists and government officials, but not by the uninformed populace living below. Lahars fifty feet (fifteen meters) high swept down from the volcano to converge in a river valley above the town of Armero, to which the government had issued a casual warning only a short time before. Families awoke to find their homes being crushed by a surging slurry of melted snow and volcanic debris. Twenty-five thousand people were killed, and many more were left homeless.

Falls of *pryoclastic* (fire-shattered) debris are part of almost every volcanic eruption. The most abundant debris ejected is ash, which is composed primarily of microscopic fragments of volcanic glass. Some eruptions produce only a light dusting of ash, while others expel it by the cubic mile. In A.D. 79, the volcano Vesuvius buried the Roman city of Pompeii under a ten-foot- (three-meter-) thick layer in the course of one day, literally smothering its 20,000 inhabitants. The following day, neighboring Herculaneum was inundated by a lahar.

The partially excavated ruins of the Roman metropolis Pompeii (below) were buried in 79 AD by volcanic debris from the nearby volcano Vesuvius (in an artist's rendition, right).

Lava originating in Hawaii's Kilauea volcano flows across the island to the sea, raising clouds of steam as it cools in the water. Note the black sand beach, composed of volcanic rock fragments.

The least dangerous and most familiar kind of volcanic eruption is the lava flow. Since magma must be depleted of volatile compounds in order to flow like a fluid, lava flows are confined to oceanic volcanoes fed by volatile-poor magma from the earth's mantle, or to areas on the continents where deep fissures have tapped the same deep sources. It is not surprising that on the Hawaiian islands only one person has been killed by lava this century, since lava rarely flows faster than a person can walk. The threat to property is considerably greater, however; Hawaii's vital port city of Hilo is presently threatened by flows from the active volcano Kilauea.

The greatest threat presented by lava lies in the poisonous gases that may issue from the earth along with the flow. The eruption of the Laki Fissure on Iceland in 1783 covered 200 square miles (520 square kilometers) with lava. Nobody was killed by the lava itself, but there was no escape from the poisonous blue pall of sulfur dioxide, carbon dioxide, and fluorine gas that clung to the island. Crops and livestock gradually died, and even the fish abandoned the island's polluted waters. The people grew sick, and eventually 10,000 died during what is still called the Hardship of the Blue Cloud.

It takes courage and ingenuity to survive on a remote, storm-lashed island in the North Atlantic, so it is not surprising that the Icelanders were the first people to fight a volcanic eruption—and win.

Off the southwest coast of Iceland lies the island of Heimay. It is blessed with one of the world's finest natural harbors, of vital importance in these stormy seas. Although small, Heimay is very important to the economy of Iceland, since a large percentage of the country's exports pass through its canneries.

Heimay has many natural wonders, not the least of which is the volcano Helgafell. On January 23, 1973, after lying dormant for 7,000 years, a gaping fissure rent the side of the volcano, passing through the outskirts of town and beneath the sea. Fountains of molten lava rose from the fissure, and lava flows began their ominous progress toward the harbor. Most of Heimay's 4,000 residents evacuated calmly over the next three hours, while volcanic ash fell like snow. As they passed through the mouth of the harbor in overcrowded fishing boats, they could see the fiery glow of the gaping fissure through the steaming water.

Many stood their ground, however, not willing to abandon their homes in the face of the slow-moving lava. A nascent volcano was threatening to form atop Iceland's most treasured harbor, and immediate action was called for. Thorbjorn Sigurgeirsson, a physics professor from the mainland, provided an ingenious idea. Thorbjorn had been on the nearby volcanic island of Surtsey while it was forming during the 1960s. There he had noticed that when small lava flows reached the coast, they sometimes turned and ran along the water's edge, the cooled and hardened side forming a dam to the molten material behind.

Working around the clock, the island's volunteer fire department sprayed the encroaching lava flows with water from the harbor, hardening their leading edge into an impenetrable wall and causing the flow to veer away from the harbor. The American air base at Keflavik supplied pipes and larger pumps, then the Navy arrived with invasion pumps originally designed to bring gasoline ashore at Omaha Beach during World War II. As each successive flow was diverted, a giant cliff rose up behind the village. In all, six million tons (five million metric tons) of water were pumped from the harbor, cooling five million cubic yards (four million cubic meters) of lava. The decision to concentrate on saving the harbor unfortunately meant sacrificing

Lava flows encroach a home (left), following the eruption of the volcano Helgafell on the Icelandic island of Heimay in 1973. Sheep looked on forlornly as their pasture was buried under ash and fountains of lava cascaded behind them (above,top). As volcanic debris rained down on the village of Heimay (above), its residents fought with tractors, firehoses, and determination to save their ancestral home.

more than 300 homes to the lava. These were pushed along, as if by a bulldozer, before crumpling and bursting into flames.

Almost six months later, the lava stopped flowing, and the inhabitants returned to an island one-fifth larger than the one they left. Homes were dug out of the ash. The people whose houses had been consumed by the lava often rebuilt on the same site—atop seventy feet (twenty-one meters) of fresh basalt. Today, pipes run into the lava field meet all of Heimay's heating needs. People dig a foot down into the ground to bake "hot spring bread." Life goes on.

There are more than 500 active volcanoes in the world today, mostly clustered on the convergent margins of the dozen tectonic plates that comprise the crust of the earth. In contrast, spreading centers are the sites where molten rock, heated and buoyed up by the radioactive decay of minerals deep within the earth, pushes apart and hardens onto the growing edges of oceanic crust. Volcanoes are common features along these mid-ocean ridges, but only rarely do they break the ocean surface, as Iceland has.

Where the dense oceanic crust collides with the lighter continental crust, the oceanic crust plunges under the continent. The descending oceanic slab is resorbed into the earth's mantle, and molten rock erupts to the surface to form volcanoes such as the Andes and the Cascades. Sometimes the varying density of oceanic crust and the imperfect geometry of the earth cause the crust to warp and thrust under itself, resulting in arcuate chains of volcanic islands such as the Aleutians, the West Indies, and Japan.

Chains of volcanoes that lie far away from spreading centers or convergent margins, such as the Hawaiian Islands, are apparently formed by isolated plumes of heat called hot spots, which rise from deep within the earth. Since hot spots are sta-

tionary, a series of volcanoes blister the plates as they pass overhead. A new volcano is growing beneath the sea southeast of Hawaii even now, while the eroded remnants of the oldest volcanoes in that chain are disappearing under the Eurasian Plate thousands of miles to the northwest. Continents pass over hot spots as well. The lava fields that cover much of Oregon and Washington and the volcanic deposits of Yellowstone National Park are thought to have formed in this way.

Where the Gorda Plate dips under the North American continent, thousands of years of volcanic eruptions have built the towering Cascades. From northern California to British Columbia march an imposing series of peaks, including Mt. Shasta in California and Mt. Rainier in Washington, both over 14,000 feet (4,300 meters) high. Mt. Saint Helens was a smaller but very symmetrical volcanic cone, built by almost 40,000 years of lava flows, ash falls, and lahars in a sparsely populated corner of southwestern Washington. In the spring of 1980, after 123 years of dormancy, it rumbled to life.

On March 20, 1980, several small earthquakes rattled the mountain, followed a week later by a small eruption of ash and

steam. The United States Geological Survey (USGS) issued a hazard alert, warning residents of the area of a potentially dangerous eruption. In April, a harmonic tremor appeared on the geologists' seismographs, indicating that magma was moving inside the volcano. A bulge appeared on the northeast flank of the mountain and was soon growing six feet (1.5 meters) per day. The USGS issued another warning, and the governor of Washington ordered the evacuation of everyone within a five-mile (eight-kilometer) radius of the volcano's base.

At 8:32 a.m. on May 18, an earthquake of magnitude 5 sent the ominous bulge hurtling down the side of Mt. Saint Helens. As if a champagne cork had been popped, a tremendous *nuée ardente* issued from the gap, devastating an area twelve miles (nineteen kilometers) outward from the volcano and fifteen miles (twenty-four kilometers) wide. USGS geologist David Johnston radioed an enthusiastic final message before his observation post eight miles (thirteen kilometers) to the north was enveloped in the blast—"Vancouver, Vancouver, this is it!"

More than 1,000 feet (300 meters) blew off the top of the mountain. A huge plume of ash spread across the sky, completely obscuring the sun 150 miles (240 kilometers) to the north and east, and covering much of Washington, Idaho, and Montana with several inches of ash. An enormous lahar filled the Toutle River valley with 200 feet (sixty meters) of debris for seventeen miles (twenty-seven kilometers), disrupting shipping where it empties into the Columbia River.

Virtually all forms of life in the vicinity of the volcano were annihilated, including an estimated sixty people. Yet within a few short weeks, wildflowers could be seen tentatively emerging from the landscape of ash and mud, while deer, elk, and geologists stepped gingerly through the rubble.

8,000 foot (2,400 meter) high Mt. Mayon volcano (left) on the Philippine Island of Luzon has been active, producing lava flows, ash falls, nueé ardentes, and lahars for all of recorded history. During its last eruption in 1968, a major disaster was averted when the government evacuated some 70,000 people from villages around its base. Mt. St. Helens in Washington State (above) appears peaceful prior to its eruption on May 18, 1980. It is one of many volcanos in the Cascade Range, which stretches from Northern California into Canada. Clouds of volcanic ash and steam (right) billowed out of the crater for weeks, darkening the sky over much of the Pacific Northwest.

The eruption of Mt. St. Helens blew
1,300 feet (400 meters) off the top of the
volcano (above), leaving a jagged crater
in which a new lava dome has risen.
Thick mudflows filled the valleys surrounding the volcano (right), carrying
millions of tons of debris into the Columbia River. Like a vision of nuclear apoca-
lypse, 150 square miles (250 kilometers)
of forest was reduced to a jumble of
matchsticks by the explosion (far right).

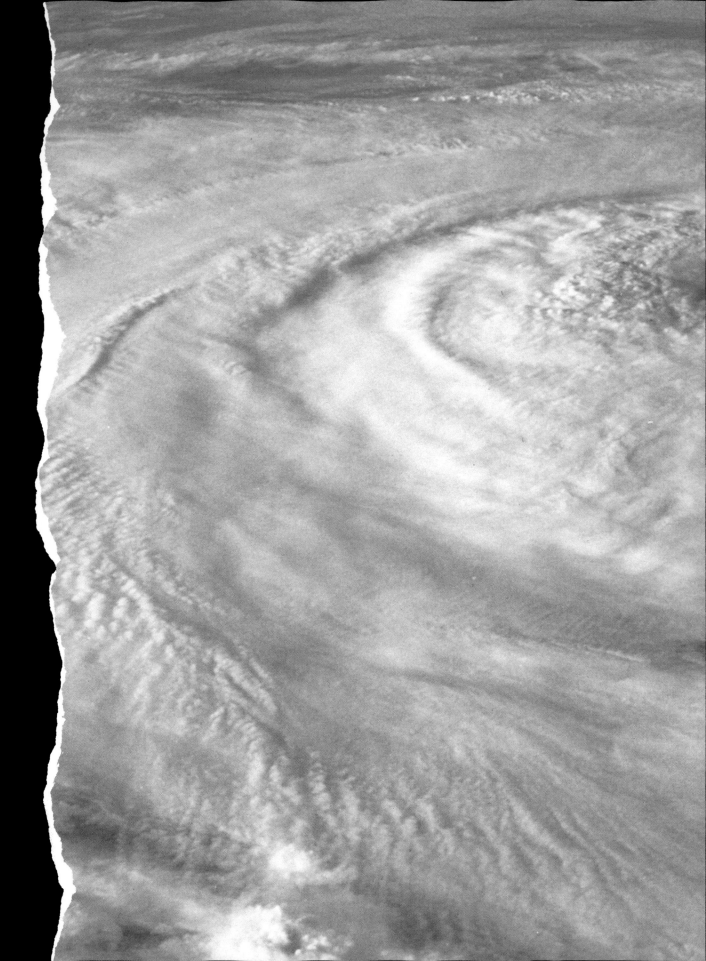

Chapter Three

TROPICAL CYCLONES

GALVESTON, TEXAS, WAS A BUSTLING boomtown at the turn of the twentieth century. Much of the Lone Star State's wealth of agricultural and mineral products was shipped from its harbor, and there was plenty of room for tourists on its long Gulf Coast beaches. Situated on a mile-wide barrier island separating the harbor from the Gulf, this prosperous city boasted many stately homes and fine buildings. Not one was built on land higher than nine feet (three meters) above sea level.

In the first week of September 1900, a tropical storm of unknown intensity stalked the Gulf of Mexico. It had swept across Cuba and Florida, but where its next landfall would be no one could predict. There were no weather satellites then, and ships at sea did not yet have the technology to radio in the positions of the storms they encountered. The National Weather Bureau in Washington telegraphed messages to the cities and towns along the Gulf Coast, warning of a possible hurricane approaching from the southeast.

On September 7, warning flags were dutifully raised over the Weather Bureau's offices in downtown Galveston. A refreshing ocean breeze picked up as the barometer began to fall, but by afternoon the increasingly violent surf had driven bathers from the beach. Throughout the night, the tide continued to rise.

By the next morning, seawater was invading beachfront homes and streets, while rain whipped across the sky. The wind increased steadily to more than seventy-five miles (120 kilometers) per hour, blowing in windows and sending slate shingles slicing through the air like boomerangs. By mid afternoon, the single bridge connecting Galveston to the mainland was lost to the rising waters, and with it all hopes of escape for the island's terrified residents.

As darkness fell, the storm surge crested at more than fifteen feet (five meters) above normal high tide. Houses that had not been demolished floated crazily about, their occupants holding on desper-

ately as they were swept out to sea. The tallest buildings downtown stood like islands amid the maelstrom of churning debris. Everywhere survivors clung to floating planks and doors, their cries for help lost in the howling wind.

Around midnight, the wind and rain subsided, and the tide gradually withdrew. Dawn revealed an apocalyptic scene: Where the city of Galveston had once stood was now a tangle of driftwood and bodies. More than 3,000 buildings, half of the city, were completely destroyed; 6,000 of its residents were killed or missing. With an equal number lost on the mainland, help was slow to arrive; it must have seemed to the survivors that the world had ended that morning.

In a truly Texas-sized effort, the survivors retrenched and rebuilt their devastated metropolis. Behind a newly constructed, three-mile- (five-kilometer-) long seawall, thousands of tons of granite and sand were piled, raising the level of the city more than fifteen feet (five meters) in

places. More than two thousand surviving structures were jacked up to the new level. These efforts to foil nature have apparently succeeded, as Galveston has survived several serious hurricanes since the nightmare of 1900.

Tropical cyclones are called hurricanes in the Western Hemisphere and typhoons in the Eastern Hemisphere, but the distinction is arbitrary. The sixty or so cyclones which form throughout the world each year are similar in most respects. They begin as areas of low atmospheric pressure over very warm equatorial seas. Winds flowing in from areas of higher pressure begin to spiral around the areas of low pressure because of the Coriolis effect, a product of the earth's rotation that tends to deflect winds to the right in the Northern Hemisphere and to the left in the Southern. Cyclones do not form in the immediate area of the equator, since the Coriolis force only takes effect above 5° latitude.

Humid air from the warm ocean infuses the growing cyclone with moisture. As this

A neighborhood in Galveston, Texas, (bottom left) was reduced to driftwood by the great hurricane of 1900. With orders to shoot looters on sight, a vigilante stands guard (bottom right). However, most people were only interested in finding family members and friends amid the wreckage of the beleaguered city, where one person in six was killed by the storm.

Hurricane Gilbert prowls the Caribbean in this NASA satellite image (below). Note the characteristic spiral structure of the storm and the clear eye at its center, an area of relatively calm winds and intense low pressure.

© Warren Faidley

moisture condenses to form rain, a tremendous amount of energy is released, driving the winds to draw more moisture into the storm. The average diameter of tropical cyclones is between 100 and 200 miles (160 and 320 kilometers), with a central region of relative calm air and clear skies called the *eye* up to ten miles (sixteen kilometers) across. Winds may be felt 500 miles (800 kilometers) away from the storm itself.

The average tropical cyclone lasts less than ten days and covers up to 2,000 miles (3,200 kilometers). They are usually extinguished by the loss of a humid air source, though they have been known to travel long distances over land. In 1969, for ex-

ample, Hurricane Camille swept across the South from Louisiana to Virginia, raining furiously the entire distance.

There are several major regions where the conditions that give rise to cyclones exist. The most prolific is in the Western Pacific, east of the Phillipine Islands, from which as many as twenty typhoons per year may move northward to the South China Sea or Japan. The most severe cyclones originate in the Bay of Bengal, east of India, during the late spring and fall. Inundating the densely populated and very low-lying Ganges Delta with fifteen foot (five meter) tidal surges, these typhoons never fail to take a staggering human toll.

Over 200 people were killed when Hurricane Camille roared out of the Gulf of Mexico in 1969, pounding the Mississippi Delta region with winds up to 200 miles (320 kilometers) per hour. The high winds swept the ocean right through Biloxi, Mississippi (left), depositing fishing vessels in front yards and automobiles on the beach (above).

Storm surges, the exceptionally high tides driven by a hurricane's winds (opposite page) cause severe damage in coastal areas. A *chubasco* (hurricane), charged with moisture from its trip up the Gulf of California, brings unaccustomed flooding to the Arizona desert (above, bottom). Charleston, South Carolina (above, top) was turned into a ghost town when Hurricane Hugo tore through it in 1989, destroying entire neighborhoods, but failing to dampen the locals' sense of humor. Before reaching the Carolina Coast, Hugo unleashed its fury on the Caribbean; on the island of Guadeloupe (overleaf) a tourist resort is beset by the rising flood waters and gale-force winds.

The typhoon of November 13, 1970, killed between 500,000 and 1,000,000 people, making it the single worst disaster of the century.

Cyclones also originate in a broad area south of the equator, between Fiji in the Pacific all the way across the top of Australia and into the Indian Ocean. These storms commonly move south into Australia, where they are disrespectfully called Willy-Willies.

Late summer hurricanes like the one that ravaged Galveston usually form in the open ocean between the West Indies and Africa, then travel west toward Mexico or the Gulf Coast. Early summer and fall hurricanes often originate in the Caribbean or the Gulf and may move northward along the Eastern seaboard.

Elsewhere in the Western Hemisphere, hurricanes form off the west coast of Mexico, where they are called *chubascos*. Chubascos commonly travel up the narrow Gulf of California, strengthened by its very warm waters. They usually pass over the peninsula of Baja California and out to sea, but occasionally continue up into the deserts of California or Arizona to cause massive flooding.

In 1954, three major hurricanes, Carol, Edna, and Hazel, devastated the eastern United States, causing an estimated one billion dollars in damage. The following year, two others left an even greater toll in their wake. Not coincidentally, 1955 saw the establishment of the National Hurricane Research Project. Today, hurricanes are one of the most exhaustively studied of atmospheric phenomena.

Hurricanes were given female names by meteorologists between 1953 and 1978, on the theory that these names were more pleasing to the ear. To many people, however, this quaint naming custom seemed more like a chauvanistic comment on female nature, and in 1978 tropical cyclones went coed.

TORNADOES

ON MARCH 18, 1925, A LARGE THUNderstorm rumbled across southeastern Missouri, lashing Reynolds County with driving rain and hail. Shortly after noon, the air grew still and the sky took on a peculiar greenish cast, while the clouds continued to roil and churn overhead. A dark fang gradually dipped down from the leading edge of the storm, toward the stubble-filled fields below: the nascent vortex of what was to become the deadliest tornado in history. Within minutes, the twister had claimed its first victims, devastating the town of Annapolis.

Rushing northeast at sixty miles (ninety-six kilometers) per hour, the tornado grew into a thundering juggernaut more than a mile wide, darkened by swirling debris and pierced by bolts of lightening. Tearing through southern Illinois, the tornado flung bodies into the forests and fields a mile and more from its path as it swept up farmhouses and leveled much of four towns. Crossing the Wabash River into Indiana, it left just four buildings standing out of the two hundred that had once been the town of Griffin. In nearby Princeton, the devastation was so spectacular that tourists came flocking by the thousands as soon as the dust had cleared.

Sated at last, the tornado dissipated into the evening sky. In its three-and-a-half-hour rampage, what became known as the Tri-State Tornado had left a swath of destruction 219 miles (350 kilometers) long and had taken nearly 700 lives.

Although unusual in its magnitude, the Tri-State Tornado was spawned by the same conditions that produce more than 700 smaller tornadoes every year in the United States alone. Covering distances of five to fifteen miles (eight to twenty-four kilometers) in an average of five minutes or less, these tornadoes take a cumulative toll of more than two hundred lives per year—a threat second only to lightning among natural phenomena. Tornadoes occur

A tornado churns across the fields of Elbert County, Colorado (left). A tornado that tore through Maple Grove, Minnesota, pulled household items through windows, then picked up a home and parked it on top of a car (right and below).

Tornados are by no means confined to land. Waterspouts, such as the one at left, constitute a rare but potent threat to marine traffic and may move inland to become tornados. The complete destruction of these homes in Saragosa, Texas (right) graphically illustrates the awesome violence of some tornados.

when the distribution of temperature and humidity in the atmosphere is thrown out of balance; the Tri-State tornado, for example, apparently arose when a fast-moving tropical storm from the Gulf of California encountered a cold front over the western plains.

These conditions are frequently encountered in the midwestern United States in the spring (and to a lesser extent in the fall), when humid cyclones and thunderstorms swing northward to collide with the cool, dry air over the continent. Tornadoes formed in this region usually travel toward the northeast, apparently steered by the jet stream. Kansas and Oklahoma lie at the heart of what has been called *tornado alley*. This broad sweep of plains between the Mississippi River and the Rocky Mountains, extending north from the Gulf Coast into Canada, is by far the most tornado-prone region on earth. The threat diminishes gradually toward the Eastern seaboard, and is practically nonexistent west of the Rocky Mountains.

Since the geographic distribution of tornadoes clearly favors flat regions, it is not surprising that they form over the oceans as well. *Waterspouts,* as marine tornadoes are called, are particularly common in the tropics, but can occur anywhere that thunderstorms develop over the water. Although primarily a hazard to navi-

gation, waterspouts have moved inland to become deadly tornadoes.

Because they are violent and sporadic, tornadoes are among the most difficult atmospheric phenomena to study, and their dynamics are still poorly understood. Different researchers support several competing theories. It is fairly certain that tornadoes are fed by the strong updrafts associated with violent thunderstorms, and that wind shear has a role in initiating their rotation. Since tornadoes are almost always accompanied by intense lightning, some scientists have suggested that they may be driven in part by the heat of this electrical discharge.

The characteristic funnel cloud first becomes visible as the air inside it expands and cools under the reduced pressure, causing droplets of water to condense. The tornado may be darkened further as soil and debris are inhaled by updraft winds approaching 200 miles (320 kilometers) per hour. Since the air pressure within a tornado can be 10 percent lower than the ambient atmospheric pressure, a closed building in the path of a fast-moving tornado may explode from decompression as if struck by a bomb. Much more damage, however, is done by the incredible winds tornadoes generate, capable of driving splinters through metal posts or tossing eighty-five-ton (seventy-seven-metric-ton)

© Photri

The funnel cloud characteristic of most tornados (above) becomes visible as moisture condenses inside the intense vacuum and soil and debris are sucked inside. The extreme low pressure that suddenly enveloped this Texas mobile home (right) apparently caused it to burst apart. The contents of another mobile home in Valparaiso, Texas (far right) lies strewn about in the wake of a tornado.

© Lee Langum/FPG International

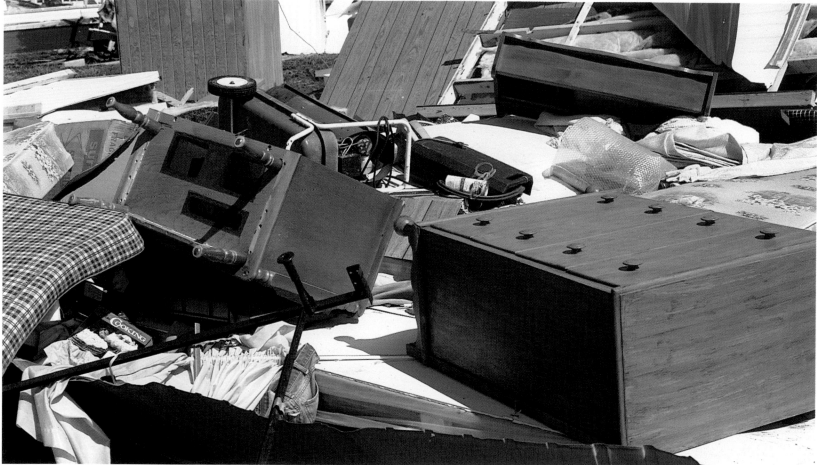

railroad cars into the air. At over 300 miles (480 kilometers) per hour, these are the highest surface winds known.

Regional weather patterns sometimes conspire to produce scores of tornadoes simultaneously over a vast area. The so-called Superoutbreak of 1974 is an extraordinary example. Between the time the first tornado was sighted in Illinois on April 3, and the last one dissipated in North Carolina the next day, 148 tornados ravaged thirteen states in the Midwest and the South. Although almost 30,000 homes were destroyed, only 315 people lost their lives, because there had been early warnings and evacuations. The similar Enigma Outbreak of 1884, although smaller than the 1974 disaster, struck without warning

and claimed more than twice as many lives.

On days when the National Weather Service believes that atmospheric conditions are ripe for tornadoes, the Radio Emergency Associated Citizens Team (REACT) is activated throughout the threatened area. These volunteer ham and citizens band radio operators station themselves with their radios at vantage points to watch for developing funnel clouds. If a tornado is spotted, the authorities are alerted and warnings are broadcast over the air. Since tornadoes tend to follow fairly straight paths, these advisories are usually effective in getting the right people evacuated or into shelters. Many residents of tornado-prone regions purchase special transmitters, which sit quietly

on the mantle until activated by a National Weather Service broadcast, whereupon they emit an irritating warning signal.

Scientists at the University of Oklahoma's National Severe Storms Laboratory actually leap into their cars and chase tornadoes when such warnings are issued. These extremely dedicated researchers have designed a device which they hope will dispel some of the tornado's mystery: the Totable Tornado Observatory, or TOTO. After being placed in the path of an oncoming twister, TOTO is supposed to record the wind speed and direction, the air pressure and temperature, and the strength of the electrical field within the tornado funnel. If not destroyed or whisked off to Oz, that is.

Chapter Five
EL NIÑO

THE TRADE WINDS BLOW ALMOST constantly along the northwest coast of South America, sweeping down through the foothills of the Andes to flock the rolling Pacific with whitecaps. Millions of seabirds wheel and glide on the wind, plunging into the waves to gorge themselves on vast schools of fish. The wind is largely responsible for this great abundance of life. It literally pushes the surface water away from the shoreline, allowing cool, nutrient-rich deep water to rise in its place. Although the incessant offshore wind has made a desert of the coastal region, it has more than compensated by providing Ecuador and Peru with the world's greatest fishery.

Near the end of each year, the winds gradually diminish. As the upwelling ceases, the fish begin to disperse, and the temperature of the ocean surface rises. The equatorial sun beats down upon the stagnant sea, and rainclouds mass and move inland, bringing torrential rains. Since this phenomenon usually begins around Christmas and departs before Easter, local fisherman long ago named it *El Niño,* after the Christ Child. El Niño has made its annual visitation since time immemorial, and the people it affects have learned how to live with it. Every few years, however, the Child is very bad indeed, lingering for months. The seas grow ever warmer as the rains continue to fall, washing away roads and homes and sometimes entire towns.

In September 1982, the fishermen in the coastal villages of Peru could feel the wind on their faces as they stood looking out to sea. The trade winds had subsided weeks before, and now a strange westerly wind had begun to blow. Although the fishermen knew from long experience that hard times lay ahead, they had no idea that the worst El Niño in history was brewing. The sea would remain barren for nearly a year, and hundreds of people in Ecuador and Peru would be swept away by floods and landslides. Unsuspected by anyone, the weather of the entire planet was slowly slipping into chaos. Before it ended halfway through the following year, floods, fires, droughts, and cyclones would take countless lives and inflict billions of dollars worth of damage around the world.

Halfway around the world in India, farmers gazed patiently into the clear blue skies, waiting for rain. The wait would be a long one. Farmers throughout southern Asia depend upon the monsoon winds to gather the rain clouds from over the Indian

© Daily Telegraph/International Stock Photos

Ocean and carry them over their fields and paddies. Every few years, however, the rains fail to appear. As their crops wither and die, millions of people already on the margins of survival are beset by famine.

The colonial authorities in India were appalled by this unpredictable and potentially volatile state of affairs. After the region was again plunged into drought in 1899, the British decided that some means must be found to reliably forecast the monsoon's failure. This mission fell to the mathematician Gilbert Walker, appointed as India's director of observatories. Walker studied the monsoon for decades, poring over weather records from around the globe in an attempt to discern some pattern to its behavior. Although he was never able to render a reliable forecast, Walker did make an invaluable discovery. He observed that atmospheric pressure was usually high over the Pacific Ocean and low over the Indian Ocean, and that the monsoon failed when this relationship spontaneously reversed. Walker called his discovery the Southern Oscillation—unaware that the fishermen of South America already knew it as El Niño.

Meteorologists are very interested in atmospheric pressure, since it controls the distribution of rain and wind around the world. Regions of low pressure tend to produce rain clouds, while skies are clear in high-pressure areas; winds prefer to flow from high pressure to low. Over the oceans, surface water temperatures tend to control the distribution of pressure systems. Above warm, tropical seas, the air grows warmer and expands, rising and diffusing outward so that atmospheric pressure is decreased. Cold waters, on the other hand, cool the overlying air and increase its density, creating high pressure regions. These simple observations help meterologists understand how global weather sytems work, and how disturbances such as El Niño occur.

Under normal conditions, the cold upwelling waters off the coast of South America give rise to high atmospheric pressure over the eastern Pacific, while the warm waters of the western Pacific and Indian oceans breed low pressure and tropical storms. The trade winds flow from the high in the east toward the low in the west. Since these winds cause the upwelling of cold water in the eastern Pacific, and constantly push the warm surface waters into the western Pacific, they sustain this pressure gradient. It has been clear for many years that El Niño, or the Southern Oscillation, occurs when this system breaks down, but only recently have scientists been able to explain why.

© Herman J. Kokojan/Black Star

© Anthony Suau/Black Star

A severe El Niño can affect the weather of the entire planet. Typhoons (opposite page) are unusually plentiful in El Niño years, spreading destruction throughout the South Pacific and Far East. Meanwhile, rivers swollen by torrential rains inundate the Southeastern United States (above). At left, farmers in Bangladesh inspect the sodden remains of their meager crops. Denied the vital monsoon rains by El Niño during 1987, freak floods arrived late in the season to wash away their harvests and homes.

© Lee Langum/FPG International

Among the effects of El Niño on the United States are unusually heavy rains or snowfall in the South and West, which can cause devastating floods such as this one in a suburb of Jackson, Mississippi (far left). Overcorrection of oceanic and atmospheric circulation patterns following the El Niño may bring on a reverse effect called *La Niña*, which can cause severe drought in the same regions a few months later (right).

Researchers at Columbia University in New York City have created sophisticated new computer models, which use formulas describing the physics of the ocean and atmosphere to simulate these natural processes. Like armchair quarterbacks watching an instant replay, they can see exactly where things began to go wrong as the simulation unfolds. It seems that even while normal conditions prevail, the volume of warm surface water in the equatorial Pacific is gradually increasing. When a critical point is reached, warm water begins to make inroads into the region of upwelling along the South American coast. The intrusion is small, but sufficient enough to weaken the high pressure system and cause the trade winds to falter. This is the point at which El Niño begins.

The collapse of the trade winds allows the warm water confined to the western Pacific to flood back eastward. It travels at a speed of about 150 miles (240 kilometers) per day in *Kelvin waves,* a sort of constant tidal progression that gains momentum from the Earth's rotation. As surface temperatures decline, the Indo-Pacific low begins to deteriorate, spelling doom for the monsoon. In about two month's time, warm water reaches the coast of South America, bringing with it El Niño. Now that the high and low pressure systems have reversed, easterly winds begin to develop.

With no resistance from the trade winds, Kelvin waves continue to migrate eastward, transporting ever-cooler surface water into the eastern Pacific. When the reservoir of warm water gathered against South America is finally dispersed, normal conditions are restored. Sometimes the western Pacific loses too much heat in this exchange, causing a sort of reverse El Niño, which wags have dubbed *La Niña* (the girl). Some researchers believe that a rapid cooling that followed the 1986–1987 El Niño was responsible for a subsequent drought in the American Midwest and concurrent flooding in Bangladesh.

El Niño of 1982–1983 was the most violent climatic upheaval of this century, affecting the weather of every continent but Europe and Antarctica. The trade winds first began to collapse in May 1982, and by July the oscillation of pressure systems across the Pacific was complete. In southern Asia, mudcracks spread across the desiccated rice paddies as rain clouds were drawn away to dissipate over the ocean. Indonesia's already strained resources became tragically overdrawn as hundreds died of starvation. Australia lost half of its vital grain crop, but that was only the start of the troubles down under.

Australia's reservoirs and streams dried up one by one as the summer wore on. With their natural forage shriveling under the relentless sun, kangaroos swarmed like locusts over the few remaining crops and stock tanks. Cattle and sheep perished by the thousands and had to be bulldozed

© Ron Ryan/Sygma

© David Austen/Black Star

© David Austen/Black Star

into makeshift mass graves. On February 8, hot winds swept the parched soil of South Australia into a 300-mile- (480-kilometer-) wide dust storm, burying the city of Melbourne under half a million tons of fine grit.

Scorching winds of up to seventy miles (110 kilometers) per hour continued to torment Melbourne and Adelaide, as the temperatures rose to 110°F (40°C) and the humidity sank to 10 percent. On February 18, Ash Wednesday, fires began to break out in the tinder-dry bush. The resinous leaves of the native eucalyptus began to emit explosive vapors in the heat, bursting into flame as the brushfires approached. Racing through the treetops, the fires consumed entire towns despite the efforts of volunteer firefighters. By the time the fires subsided, 2,000 square miles had been reduced to cinders, seventy-five people were dead, and 8,000 were left homeless.

The intense El Niño of 1983 brought a withering drought to Australia, turning pasture lands to desert and forests into kindling. There was little anyone could do as fire swept across southern Australia (opposite page), consuming everything in its path. For as long as they could afford to, cattle and sheep ranchers (above) trucked dwindling supplies of feed and water to their starving herds.

The Society Islands in Polynesia rarely suffer more than one cyclone every few years, but El Niño brought in a bounty of six over a five-month period. Typhoon Veena was the worst cyclone Tahiti had ever experienced, displacing 25,000 people in the wake of its fierce gales and tidal surges. Another of the dozens of cyclones that swarmed the Pacific Basin, Typhoon Iwa slammed into Hawaii in November, causing millions of dollars in damage.

El Niño had a number of surprises in store for North America as well. The low pressure system in the Gulf of Alaska, where much of the North Pacific's foul weather begins, was greatly intensified. Perturbations of the jet stream sent large storms wandering off their normal courses to batter the coast of California. Enormous and uninvited storm waves muscled their way through the back doors of Malibu's million-dollar homes, while elsewhere tor-

© C. Simonpietri/Sygma

Although El Niño is not confined to the Pacific Ocean, some of its worst effects occur there. Nobody in Tahiti lives far from the sea, which is why Typhoon Veena caused such complete destruction there (left and inset). In Southern California, people who live on the beach are usually envied—except in El Niño years. Above, homes on California's Central Coast collapse into the sea during one of the unusually violent storms of January 1983.

rential rains sent whole neighborhoods sliding downhill. All along the West Coast, commercial fishermen were distraught to find strange, warm-water species in their nets, while their accustomed quarry was nowhere to be found. Soon after their customers developed a passion for swordfish and mahimahi, these fish disappeared again.

As skiers in the Rocky Mountains enjoyed record snowfalls, the southeastern states were literally swamped with rain. Streets became canals in low-lying Gulf Coast towns, as the Mississippi and other

rivers flooded their levees to cause millions of dollars worth of property damage. Families paddled off in rowboats to visit relatives on higher ground, while catfish explored their abandoned living rooms. Fortunately, there was no threat from hurricanes. The 1982–1983 season saw fewer hurricanes develop in the Atlantic and Caribbean than during any year in the previous fifty.

The impact of El Niño on Africa is more difficult to estimate, but it was certainly worse than all of its other effects combined. South of the Sahara Desert lies a vast band of marginal land called the *Sa-*

hel, which stretches from Mauritania on the Atlantic eastward to Ethiopia on the Indian Ocean. As in much of southern Asia, the summer rainfall on which Sahel relies is carried by winds that are easily disrupted by the Southern Oscillation. In 1982 and 1983, virtually no rain fell in this region, setting the stage for the famine of the following year in which an estimated two million people perished. As starving livestock stripped the land of its last vestiges of vegetation, winds swept down from the Sahara to carry away the few small patches of arable soil, assuring that a legacy of hunger would endure for years. Rain finally returned to the Sahel late in 1985, but millions of people remain at the mercy of its fickle climate.

The enormous toll in human lives and property exacted by El Niño has inspired a concerted effort among meterologists to predict its recurrences. Fortunately, modern science is better equipped to undertake this task than Gilbert Walker was. Using the computer model described earlier, scientists at Columbia University predicted in early 1986 that a strong El Niño would occur by the middle of the year, and subside in early 1987. El Niño did indeed arrive, but not before October; furthermore, it persisted much longer than expected. These researchers are presently refining and improving their model of the ocean-atmosphere system, including formulas that represent such subtleties as relative humidity and the effects of the earth's topography on wind patterns. With fair warning, the world of the not-too-distant future may be prepared to face disasters head-on, realizing Gilbert Walker's dream at last.

The 1983 El Niño dealt a *coup de grace* to sub-Saharan Africa. At right, Ethiopians whose crops and livestock have been ravaged by drought wait patiently for supplies from a relief agency. In Niger, hot winds winnow the soil from the overgrazed countryside (inset).

© J. White/Black Star

INDEX

Page numbers in italics refer to captions and illustrations.